Something's Fishy

by Sue Walker
illustrated by Janine Dawson

Blake
EDUCATION
Better ways to learn

Characters

Sam

Fish
Face

Contents

Chapter 1

The Box

Sam sat in front of the television. He clicked the remote control once. He clicked it twice. Then he clicked it again. Boring news. Boring ads. Boring movies.

Sam stared out the window. Big, splotchy drops of rain battered against the glass. He punched the cushion beside him and shuffled his feet as he glanced around the room.

Sam watched Moby swim slowly across the fish tank. The water was so murky he looked as if he was swimming in honey.

Dad called Sam from the kitchen. "I know what you can do today," he said. "You can clean up your room."

Sam punched the cushion again. Was he kidding? Cleaning your room was more boring than ironing underwear. It was more boring than picking fluff off your jumper with tweezers.

"Yeah, later," said Sam. Like next year.

Dad put the dishes into the dishwasher. "Well, perhaps you could answer the doorbell for me. Can't you hear it?"

Sam could hear it, but he didn't get up. He stared at the television and a creature with a face like a fish stared back at him.

"Listen to your father," said Fish Face. "Answer the door!"

Sam blinked at the television. "Are you talking to me?" he whispered.

"Who else would I be talking to?" answered Fish Face.

Sam sprang up from the lounge and strode to the front door. His hand rested on the knob as the doorbell rang again. He looked through the peephole, but he couldn't see a thing.

Sam opened the door. The sky thundered. Rain poured. He looked left and right. Nothing! Then he looked up and down.

At the bottom of the steps was a box covered in shiny, orange paper. Rain pelted Sam as he stooped and picked it up. He squinted and read the tag. In tiny, orange letters was one word: 'Sam'.

He grinned. Maybe today wasn't going to be so boring after all.

Sam stepped back inside and closed the door. He turned the box over in his hands and shook it. It felt empty.

Sam brought the box to his ear and listened. A tiny, muffled sound came from inside.

Sam couldn't wait. He ripped off the shiny paper and flipped open the lid.

A tall figure instantly rose from the box. Sam leapt backwards and hid behind the coat rack.

Chapter 2

Make a Wish

Standing in the hallway was an orange creature with hands and feet like flippers. It had big, goggly eyes and scales that glistened like sequins.

It was Fish Face, from the television. "So, what's your wish?" Fish Face asked.

Sam swallowed. "Huh?"

"You get one wish," said Fish Face.

Sam peeked out from behind the coats. This was weird. Weirder than weird. "Where did you come from?" he asked.

A bubble escaped from Fish Face's mouth.

"You called me," said Fish Face impatiently.

"You keyed my number into the TV remote control. So here I am."

"Oh, right," said Sam. He nodded as if he understood.

"So, give me your wish, and make it snappy."

"Okay," said Sam, thinking fast. "Um ... I wish for the most unboring day ever."

11

Fish Face bowed slowly. He looked Sam in the eyes, slapped his fins once and vanished — box and all.

"Are you ready?" asked a voice behind Sam.

Sam jumped and spun around. It was Fish Face, only he looked different. He had a wild look in his eyes and he was dressed in white pyjamas. Wrapped around his waist was a black belt.

Sam looked him up and down. "Err ... ready for what? Bed?"

Fish Face smacked his lips together. "Ready for your wish, of course," said Fish Face. "It's time for the most unboring day ever."

Sam grinned. This was going to be good. He looked around and sniffed the air. A strong odour filled his nostrils. "Do you smell something?" asked Sam.

Fish Face inhaled. "Like what?"

"Like fi... "

The air vibrated. Sam's eyes blurred. An orange light flashed. Sam was gone!

Sam stood on a huge, padded floor. A crowd roared around him. Thousands of people sat on rows of seats. All of them stared at Sam. Sam's eyes opened wide. He felt cold. Where was he?

Fish Face crossed the mat. He had that wild look in his eyes. He raised his flippers and the crowd cheered and stamped their feet. Then there was silence.

A voice over the loudspeaker said, "Round One. Sam versus Fish Face."

Now Sam realised why Fish Face was wearing pyjamas. Only they weren't pyjamas.

Sam gulped. Then he gulped again.

Fish Face strode towards him, his flippers slapping the floor. Sam's eyes darted left and right. What was Fish Face doing?

"I will demonstrate O-goshi," said Fish Face. He moved up close to Sam.

Sam opened his mouth. "What's O...?"

Fish Face grabbed Sam and lifted him into the air. He slammed Sam onto the floor in one swift move. Sam groaned and stared up at Fish Face.

"That's O-goshi," said Fish Face. He bowed and backed away.

Sam listened again to the voice on the loudspeaker. "Round Two. Sam versus Giant Jim." He lifted his head and stared across the mat. Giant Jim waved his giant arms in the air. "Oh my goshi," said Sam. "No way."

Giant Jim bounded towards Sam like a grizzly bear. Sam scrambled to his feet and braced himself. He inhaled a deep, calming breath that tasted strangely of sardines.

The air vibrated. Sam's eyes blurred. An orange light flashed. Sam disappeared!

Chapter 3

A Wild Ride

The tiny car teetered at the top of the track. Sam shook his head and blinked. Then he swallowed. "Oh-oh, a roller-coaster," Sam whispered. He glanced sideways at Fish Face. He had that crazy look in his eyes again.

Fish Face threw his fins in the air and Sam gripped the bar in front of him.

The car plummeted into a deep tunnel and then shot skyward like a bullet. Fish Face laughed all the way, but Sam screamed. His eyes were fixed on the triple loop ahead. Sam's muscles tensed. His teeth clenched.

Sam hung upside down once. Then he hung upside down again.

By the third loop, Sam's face was white. The car rocketed around and Sam's stomach went topsy-turvy.

A horrid taste crept up in his throat. Sam covered his mouth with both hands.

The roller-coaster skidded to a stop. Fish Face lifted the bar and stepped onto the wooden platform. Sam couldn't move. He was still thinking about the triple loop.

Fish Face grinned. "Ahhh, that was fun. So, you want another turn?" he asked.

Before Sam had a chance to reply, Fish Face said, "Wonderful. So do I." Fish Face slapped his fins together and slid in beside Sam again. He pulled the bar down over their laps and the car shot forward. It gathered speed and Sam gulped big breaths — big, prawn-scented breaths.

The air vibrated. Sam's eyes blurred. An orange light flashed. Sam was gone!

Chapter 4

Water Worries

A river lapped gently at Sam's ankles. He turned around slowly. He held his breath and checked. No Giant Jim. No roller-coaster. Just a boat and lots of calm, blue water. Sam exhaled and smiled.

He watched the water ripple around him. Suddenly, a head appeared from the boat — an orange, fishy head.

Fish Face handed Sam two oars. "Start paddling," he said.

"This looks like fun," said Sam. He buckled his life jacket and climbed into the boat with Fish Face.

Sam dipped the oars into the water and pulled slowly. The boat glided away from the bank and headed downstream. Sam watched birds flutter on the banks. He saw dragonflies skim across the water. Sam barely had to paddle because the current moved them along gently.

"Where's that noise coming from?" he asked Fish Face. Sam could hear a kind of whooshing sound. He rowed around the bend in the river. And then he stopped.

Sam dropped the oars and clutched the sides of the boat. White water rushed around them. The boat lurched over rapids. It veered around rocks and branches. Worst of all, it filled with water.

Sam's ankles were wet. His clothes were soaked. Fish Face grinned. His scales flashed in the sunlight. He had that wild look in his eyes.

Sam heard a roaring sound. "What's that noise?" he yelled. He looked up at the sky. "It can't be thunder, there aren't any clouds."

"Why, don't you know?" asked Fish Face calmly. "It's a waterfall."

"What!" screamed Sam. He looked downstream and his skin prickled. He could see water and rocks, and then ... nothing. Sam grabbed the oars and paddled hard.

He paddled backwards. He paddled sideways. He paddled in circles.

Waves washed into the boat from every direction. No matter how hard Sam paddled, the boat still lurched downstream.

"Waterfall!" screamed Sam.

"Yes, I know," said Fish Face. He stood up in the boat like a surfer riding a wave. "I do hope you enjoy your swim," he said. Then he winked at Sam and leapt towards the bank like a flying fish.

Fish Face landed gracefully on the rocks and called to Sam. "You'll find the water very refreshing! Hang on!" he yelled, from the safety of the bank.

Sam's knuckles turned white. The waterfall roared and a mist filled the air — a strange, tuna-scented mist.

"I aaaammm!" yelled Sam.

The air vibrated. Sam's eyes blurred. An orange light flashed.

Sam stared at the ground far below. The trees looked like tiny tufts of grass. The houses looked like matchboxes. The sound of engines filled Sam's ears and he glanced sideways at Fish Face. He had that wild look in his eyes again.

"We'll be on the front page of the paper," said Fish Face.

"What do you mean?" asked Sam.

Chapter 5

Front-page News

"What do you mean?" repeated Sam nervously.

Fish Face didn't answer. Instead, he took Sam by the arm and led him to the open doorway. Sam watched the copilot put a parachute on Fish Face. Sam's heart banged in his chest. His eyes clamped shut. Straps tightened over his shoulders and something slimy rubbed against his face.

The copilot yelled in his ear, "One ... two ... three ... JUMP!"

Sam was propelled from the plane. Wind whistled past his ears and he opened his eyes. The trees grew bigger. The houses grew bigger. The ground rushed towards him. "Pull the cord!" screamed Sam.

"It's too early," said Fish Face.

"PULL THE CORD!" yelled Sam.

"Not yet," said Fish Face.

"THE TREES!" hollered Sam.

"Yes, they are lovely," said Fish Face. "I believe they're pines."

Air whipped at Sam's hair. It rushed up Sam's nostrils and he smelled salmon.

Fish Face yanked the rip cord and Sam closed his eyes.

Sam felt a thump. Sam felt a bump. Then he heard something rip.

"Whoops. Too late," said Fish Face.

Sam opened his eyes and stood still. Clothes and toys littered the carpet around him. He scanned the room and let out a deep breath. Sam was in his own bedroom.

Dad knocked on the door and opened it. "Dinner time, Sam," he said.

Sam yawned. "I'm too tired for dinner," he said. "I'm going to bed."

Dad placed a hand across Sam's forehead. "Are you feeling okay?" he asked.

"I'll be fine tomorrow," said Sam.

Sam changed into his favourite pyjamas and pulled back the covers. He collapsed onto his bed. His arms ached. His head pounded. His legs burned. In fact, everything hurt.

The soft blankets soothed him like a warm bath. His pillow felt as soft as a marshmallow.

Sam relaxed and soon he was in a deep sleep.

The next morning, Sam climbed out of bed and shuffled to the lounge room. He felt better. Much better.

He looked out the window. Big drops of rain battered against the glass and Sam smiled. Then suddenly, his smile disappeared.

He pressed his face to the fish tank and stared hard at Moby. Moby stopped swimming and stared hard at Sam. Two unblinking, goggly eyes held his gaze.

A familiar odour engulfed Sam and the hairs on the back of his neck bristled.

"Good morning," Dad said from the kitchen. "Feeling better?"

Sam turned. "Do you smell something, Dad?" he asked.

Dad sniffed the air. "Like what?"

"Like ... like ..." Sam took a deep breath. "Like fish," he said.

Sam waited.

The air didn't vibrate. His eyes didn't blur. No orange light flashed. Nothing.

Dad grinned. "Oh, that's lunch cooking. I went fishing this morning." He looked out the window at the rain. "You know, it's a perfect day to clean your room."

Sam nodded. "Yep. Great idea," he said.

He looked at Moby and winked. "And I think I'll clean Moby's room, too."

Glossary

braced
prepared for something

bristled
stood up

goggly
with eyes sticking out

make it snappy
do it quickly

murky
dark and gloomy

propelled
pushed forward

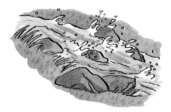

rapids
part of a river where the water flows quickly over rocks

splotchy
spotted

veered
turned another way

versus
against

Sue Walker

Once we had a fish named Sharkie. We left him at home while we went on holidays.

But when we returned, Sharkie wasn't in his cave or behind the weeds. We searched every corner of his tank. Sharkie had vanished. He'd disappeared without a trace!

Since then, I've often wondered what happened to Sharkie.

Maybe he went on an un-boring adventure? ? ?

Janine Dawson